Compiled by Andrea Skevington
This edition copyright © 2016 Lion Hudson

Published by Lion Books
an imprint of
Lion Hudson plc
Wilkinson House, Jordan Hill Road, Oxford OX2 8DR, England
www.lionhudson.com/lionchildrens

ISBN 978 0 7459 7663 1

First edition 2016

Acknowledgments

Every effort has been made to trace and contact copyright owners for material used in this book. We apologize for any inadvertent omissions or errors.

Bible extracts are taken or adapted from the Good News Bible © 1994 published by the Bible Societies/HarperCollins Publishers Ltd UK, Good News Bible © American Bible Society 1966, 1971, 1976, 1992. Used with permission.

The Lord's Prayer (on page 82) as it appears in *Common Worship: Services and Prayers for the Church of England* (Church House Publishing, 2000) is copyright © The English Language Liturgical Consultation and is reproduced by permission of the publisher.

p. 6m: John Birch, copyright © John Birch, www.faithandworship.com; used by permission.

The following prayers are taken from *The SPCK Book of Christian Prayer*, copyright © 1995, SPCK: p. 12t "May we accept this day at your hand, O Lord" by Stanley Pritchard, p. 24t "Grant me to recognize in other men, Lord God" by Pierre Teilhard de Chardin, p. 98t "Most gracious Father, this is our home" by Hugh Blackburne. Used by permission of SPCK.

pp. 12b, 13b, 18b, 21, 22, 23t, 36b, 37, 39, 41t, 41m, 42b, 43t, 43b, 44t, 49m, 49b, 52t, 53m, 53b, 56t, 64b, 70b, 72b, 73, 74t, 80b, 102t, 104, 105, 106, 108t, 108m, 108b, 112, 113, 114t, 121t: Lois Rock, copyright © Lion Hudson.

pp. 48t, 52b, 60t, 66b, 74b, 84m, 86, 92: Mary Joslin, copyright © Lion Hudson.

p. 83t: "Gift" by R. S. Thomas from *Collected Poems: 1945–1990* published by Weidenfeld & Nicolson, copyright © 2000, the estate of R. S. Thomas. Used by permission of The Orion Publishing Group.

p. 93t: Blessed Teresa of Calcutta, used by permission.

All other unattributed prayers are by Andrea Skevington, copyright © Andrea Skevington.

Carmina Gadelica collected by Alexander Carmichael is published by Floris Books, Edinburgh.

A catalogue record for this book is available from the British Library

Printed and bound in Malaysia, March 2016, LH18

PRAYERS AND VERSES

through the Bible

COMPILED BY ANDREA SKEVINGTON

LION

Contents

ONE

BEGINNINGS

Creation

So this is how it all began: with God.

This world
Your creation
Rolled into a sphere
Packaged in sunshine
Gift-wrapped in love
Given to us
Thank you

JOHN BIRCH

For the beauty of the earth,
    For the beauty of the skies,
For the Love which from our birth
    Over and around us lies:
Christ, our God, to Thee we raise
This our Sacrifice of Praise.

FOLLIOTT S. PIERPOINT (1835–1917)

God, source of all light and life,
help us to see your hand at work
in the beauty of creation.
Help us to know that, in you,
the whole earth is holy ground.

O Lord,
Your greatness
is seen
in all
the world!

PSALM 8:9

Lord, purge our eyes to see
Within the seed a tree,
Within the glowing egg a bird,
Within the shroud a butterfly.
Till, taught by such we see
Beyond all creatures, thee
And harken to thy tender word
And hear its "Fear not; it is I".

CHRISTINA ROSSETTI (1830–94)

O God, enlarge within us the sense of fellowship
with all living things, our brothers the animals
to whom thou gavest the earth as their home in
common with us.

BASIL THE GREAT (C. 330–79)

He prayeth best, who loveth best
All things both great and small;
For the dear God who loveth us,
He made and loveth all.

SAMUEL TAYLOR COLERIDGE (1772–1834)

Our Lord and God! You are worthy
   to receive glory, honour, and power.
For you created all things,
   and by your will they were given existence
   and life.

REVELATION 4:11

Lord, because you have made me, I owe you the whole
   of my love;
because you have redeemed me, I owe you the whole
   of myself;
because you have promised so much, I owe you all
   of my being…
I am wholly yours by creation: make me all yours, too,
   in love.

St Anselm of Canterbury (c. 1033–1109)

Morning prayers

Start each day with a fresh beginning;
as if this whole world was made anew.

Motto from an Amish School in Pennsylvania

Day by day,
dear Lord, of thee
three things I pray:
to see thee more clearly,
love thee more dearly,
follow thee more nearly,
day by day.

RICHARD, BISHOP OF CHICHESTER (1197–1253)

In all my thinking and speaking and doing
  this day,
help me be loving,
help me be peaceful,
help me be kind.

Let this day, O Lord, add some knowledge or good
deed to yesterday.

LANCELOT ANDREWES (1555–1626)

May we accept this day at your hand, O Lord,
as a gift to be treasured,
a life to be enjoyed,
a trust to be kept,
and a hope to be fulfilled;
and all for your glory.

STANLEY PRITCHARD

Quietly, in the morning,
I rise and look at the sky
To watch the darkness scatter
As sunlight opens the sky.
The day lies clear before me,
All fresh and shining and new,
And then I ask God to guide me
In all that I have to do.

Lord, for tomorrow and its needs,
I do not pray;
But keep me, guide me, love me, Lord,
Just for today.

SISTER M. XAVIER (1856–1917)

This simply lovely day –
  I want to share it.
There is no beauty with which
  to compare it.
Each green, each blue,
  each changing hue –
I hardly understand
  how heav'n can spare it.

TWO

LIFE'S JOURNEY

As Abraham set off for an unknown land,
so we begin each day, and each journey,
knowing you are with us.
Bless us on our way,
and make us a blessing to those we meet.

Dear God,
Help me to find the right way to go,
even though the gate to it be narrow,
and the path difficult to walk.

BASED ON MATTHEW 7:13

There is no place where God is not,
wherever I go, there God is.
Now and always he upholds me with his power
and keeps me safe in his love.

AUTHOR UNKNOWN

Trust in God
Let nothing disturb you,
let nothing frighten you;
All things pass;
God never changes.
Patience achieves
all it strives for.
He who has God
finds he lacks nothing,
God alone suffices.

ST TERESA OF AVILA (1515–82)

I am a pilgrim
on a journey
to the place
where God is found;
every step
along that journey
is upon
God's holy ground.

As Abraham and Sarah welcomed and fed
  strangers in the heat of the day,
so may we show kindness to those we meet
  on today's journey.

Help us, like Jacob, dream of angels.
Help us, wherever we wake,
to know that you are there, too.
Help us to see with new eyes.

Family

O Loving God,
May you bless our family;
may you keep us safe from harm,
may you protect us from anger that
leads to quarrels and unhappiness,
may you help us to forgive each other.
As we go out into the world,
may we bring with us your love and your peace.

Dear Lord,
Help us to be honest and kind.
Help us to be our true selves.
Help us not to do things for our own gain,
but to work together, and learn
to put each others' needs before our own.

Dear God, bless all my family,
as I tell you each name;
and please bless each one differently
for no one's quite the same.

I give thanks for the people
who are my home:
we share a place to shelter;
we share our food;
we share our times of work
and play and rest.

May we provide one another
with love, encouragement,
respect, and wisdom:
through laughter and celebration,
through tears and troubled times.

May we be to one another
roof and walls,
floor and hearth,
windows and doors.

Dear God,
Give us the
courage to
overcome anger
with love.

As Joseph forgave his brothers, and looked for good,
give us a generous heart, that we too
may do the same.

Most gracious Father,
this is our home;
let your peace rest upon it.
  Let love abide here,
  love of one another,
  love of mankind,
  love of life itself,
  and love of God.
Let us remember that
as many hands build a house,
so many hearts make a home.

HUGH BLACKBURNE (1912–95)

Help parents to understand their children.
Help children to understand their parents.

FROM EPHESIANS 6:1–4

THREE

You Do Not Forget Us

We thank you, Lord God, that you hear the prayers
   of people who carry heavy burdens.
Thank you that you heard the prayers of the slaves
   in Egypt,
and answered them with joyful freedom.
Help us to pray for those whose lives are hard.

O God,
How long must I call for help before you listen?
How can you let this wrongdoing go on…
all the fighting and the quarrelling?
Wicked people are getting the better of good people;
it is not right, it is not fair!

I will wait quietly for God to bring justice.
Even in the middle of disaster I will be joyful,
because God is my saviour.

BASED ON THE BOOK OF HABAKKUK

Teach us, Lord,
to serve you as you deserve,
to give and not to count the cost,
to fight and not to heed the wounds,
to toil and not to seek for rest,
to labour and not to ask for any reward
save that of knowing that we do your will.

St Ignatius Loyola (1491–1556)

The burning bush

Earth's crammed with heaven,
And every common bush afire with God;
But only he who sees takes off his shoes.

Elizabeth Barrett Browning (1806–1861)

Grant us a heart wide open to all this
beauty; and save our souls from being so
blind that we pass unseeing when even the
common thornbush is aflame with your
glory, O God our creator, who lives and
reigns for ever and ever.

Walter Rauschenbusch (1861–1918)

Dear Lord,
Help us to see you today in all the ordinary things
when we walk, and talk, and play;
help us to know that the whole earth
is full of your glory,
and that the ground is holy.
Amen

The world is charged with the grandeur of God.
It will flame out, like shining from shook foil.

GERARD MANLEY HOPKINS (1844–89)

Commandments

O Lord,

I have heard your commandments.

May I worship you.

May I worship you alone.

May all I say and do show respect for your holy name.

May I honour the weekly day of rest.

May I show respect for my parents.

May I reject violence so that I never take a life.

May I learn to be loyal in friendship and so learn to
be faithful in marriage.

May I not steal what belongs to others.

May I not tell lies to destroy another person's
reputation.

May I not be envious of what others have, but may I
learn to be content with the good things you give me.

BASED ON THE TEN COMMANDMENTS, EXODUS 20

Teach me, O God,
to do what is just,
to show constant love
and to live in fellowship with you.

BASED ON MICAH 6:8

Help us to love you
with all our heart and soul and mind and strength,
and help us to do what is like it:
to love our neighbour as ourselves.

FROM MATTHEW 22:37–39

You are holy, Lord, the only God,
   and your deeds are wonderful.
You are strong.
   You are great.
   You are the Most High,
   You are almighty.
   You, holy Father are
   King of heaven and earth.
You are Three and One,
   Lord God, all good.
   You are Good, all Good, supreme Good,
   Lord God, living and true.

You are love,
   You are wisdom.
   You are humility,
   You are endurance.
   You are rest,
   You are peace.
   You are joy and gladness.
   You are justice and moderation.
   You are all our riches,
   And you suffice for us.

You are beauty.

   You are gentleness.

You are our protector,

   You are our guardian and defender.

   You are courage.

   You are our haven and our hope.

You are our faith,

   Our great consolation.

   You are our eternal life,

   Great and wonderful Lord,

   God almighty,

   Merciful Saviour.

St Francis of Assisi (c. 1181–1226)

Hope is the thing with feathers
That perches in the soul
And sings the tune without the words
And never stops at all.

EMILY DICKINSON (1830–86)

FOUR

BLESSED ARE THE PEACEMAKERS

Lord, make me an instrument of thy peace.
Where there is hatred, let me sow love;
Where there is injury, pardon;
Where there is discord, union;
Where there is doubt, faith;
Where there is despair, hope;
Where there is darkness, light;
Where there is sadness, joy.

ATTRIBUTED TO ST FRANCIS OF ASSISI (C. 1181–1226)

Dear God,
We pray for the casualties of war:
for the young and the old,
for the parents and the children;
for the birds and the animals,
for the fields and the flowers;
for the earth and the water,
for the sea and the sky.
We pray for their healing.

We pray for the people who are condemned as wicked: those who are responsible for wars and massacres and terrorism.

We pray that people of good faith will find a way to stop them.

We also pray that you and we will treat them with justice and mercy.

Christ with me, Christ before me, Christ behind me,
Christ in me, Christ beneath me, Christ above me,
Christ on my right, Christ on my left,
Christ when I lie down, Christ when I sit down,
Christ when I arise,
Christ in the heart of every man who thinks of me,
Christ in the mouth of everyone who speaks of me.

St Patrick (389–461) (adapted)

Who, then, can separate us from the love of Christ? Can trouble do it, or hardship or persecution or hunger or poverty or danger or death?

Romans 8:35

We share the earth
we share the sky
we share the shining sea
with those we trust
with those we fear:
we are God's family.

Harvest

Blessed art thou, O Lord our God, King of the universe, who bringest forth bread from the earth.

JEWISH BLESSING

O God,
You show your care for the land by sending rain;
you make it rich and fertile.
You fill the streams with water;
you provide the earth with crops.
Wherever you go there is plenty.
The whole world sings for joy.

FROM PSALM 65

Thank you, dear God, for our harvest garden.
Thank you for the seeds and the soil,
for the sun and the rain,
for the roots and the leaves and the ripening fruits.
As you have blessed us with harvest gifts, dear God,
may we bless others by sharing them.

Autumn berries
round and red:
by God's hand
the birds are fed.

All good gifts around us
Are sent from heaven above;
Then thank the Lord, O thank the Lord,
For all his love.

MATTHIAS CLAUDIUS (1740–1815),
TRANSLATED BY JANE MONTGOMERY CAMPBELL (1817–78)

Remembering the story of Ruth

Lord God,
Who saw the hunger and loneliness of Ruth and
  Naomi,
and brought them to a place of plenty, and gave them
  a home,
help us when we are lost and hungry;
help us to reach out a hand to those in need.

There's trouble in the fields, Lord,
The crops are parched and dry.
We water them with tears, Lord,
So help us, hear our cry.

There's trouble in our hearts, Lord,
The world is full of pain.
Set us to work for healing,
Send blessings down like rain.

O God,
We are all strangers in this world
and we are all travelling to your country.
So may we not treat anyone as a foreigner or an
    outsider,
but simply as a fellow human being
made in your image.

Lord, watch over refugees,
their tired feet aching.
Help them bear their heavy loads,
their bent backs breaking.
May they find a place of rest,
no fears awake them.
May you always be their guide,
never forsake them.

May we learn to appreciate different points of view:

To know that the view from the hill is
    different from the view in the valley;
the view to the east is different from the
    view to the west;
the view in the morning is different from
    the view in the evening;
the view of a parent is different from the
    view of a child;
the view of a friend is different from the
    view of a stranger;
the view of humankind is different from
    the view of God.

May we all learn to see what is good, what is true,
what is worthwhile.

O God, help us not to despise or oppose
what we do not understand.

WILLIAM PENN (1644–1718)

FIVE

QUIET WATERS

Dear Lord,
Help us value the things that really matter –
kindness, and loyalty, and goodness,
and not be taken in by surface things that don't matter
   at all.
Thank you that even when we are the youngest,
and smallest, and seem least important, you know us
   and love us.
We matter to you.

When we have problems in our lives that seem as big
   as giants,
help us to trust in you to help us, and not to be afraid.

God is my shepherd, he takes care of me.

With him, I rest in green pastures,

and he guides me by quiet waters.

He heals my soul.

He leads me on paths of goodness;

Even when I pass through the dark places,

where death overshadows me,

I will not be afraid.

For you, oh God, are always there

with me.

From Psalm 23

Friendship

Dear God,
Help me to be
a friend to
someone who
needs a friend.

MARY JOSLIN

Dear friends,
Let us love one
another, because
love comes
from God.

1 JOHN 4:7

Dear God,
Thank you for our friends. Thank you for laughter
  and sharing and kindness.
Thank you for people who like us just as we are.

As David wept for his friend Jonathan, so we are sad when parted from our friends.

Dear God,
You lend us to this world
to love one another.
Now we must say goodbye
to someone we love
and who loved us.
At this time of parting,
may they know more of your love,
and may we know more of your love.
Amen

Dear God,
I am missing someone so badly.
There is a hole in my days,
in my evenings,
in my life.
Dear God,
How can I survive the pain
of missing?

Community

I was glad when they said,
"Let us go to God's house."
Already we are near,
within Jerusalem's gates.
It is a close-together city –
people live by their neighbours –
and all the different peoples come
here to praise God.
May those who love you be secure
within these your walls;
may there be peace here.
For the sake of my brothers and sisters
and friends, I will say,
"Peace be within you."

FROM PSALM 122

As the people in Solomon's time
lived in safety, each family
with their own fig tree and vine,
give each family in our community
a safe place to live, and enough to eat
and to share.

Love your neighbour
as you love yourself.

LUKE 10:27

Dear God,
I am not ready to forgive
but I am ready to be made ready.

We will find our safety
not within encircling walls
but within a circle of friendship.

MARY JOSLIN

A new school

Do not imitate
what is bad,
but imitate
what is good.

3 John 11

Goodbye, dear old school,
Hello, bright new start.
May God guide our lives,
Head and hand and heart.

Dear God,
Help us as we learn new things. If we learn quickly
　　and easily,
may we help others to understand. If we make
　　mistakes,
may we understand what went wrong. Help us never
　　to be afraid
of new things, but to see them as an adventure.

Dear Lord,
There are so many things we could ask you for.
Today we ask for wisdom, that we may understand
  you and the world and people better.
Help us to look, and to listen, with an open mind,
  that we may learn. Help us grow in wisdom
  as we grow in years.

The skies above show the glory of God;
the heavens the work of God's hands.
They speak – day and night; they do not stop –
and they are heard where every language is spoken.
Their voice goes over all the earth;
spreading out, their words encircle it.

FROM PSALM 19

SIX

FACING DIFFICULTIES

Help in times of trouble

In the face of evil and wrongdoing
I will surely not be happy,
Nor will I let myself grow too sad.
Instead, I will choose to stand up for what is right
And I will face the future
With calm and courage and cheerfulness.

I will not worry, dear God,
but I will ask you for the things I need
and give thanks.

Give me the peace that comes from knowing
that all my worries are safe with you.

FROM PHILIPPIANS 4:6–7

Dear God,

When we hear a mighty wind, strong enough to
    shatter rock,

when the ground underneath us shakes like an
    earthquake,

when fire comes from mountains,

help us to know these sounds of power and anger are
    not your voice.

Help us to listen in the silence for your whisper.

Help us to wait for your whisper.

God is our shelter and strength,
    always ready to help in times of trouble.

So we will not be afraid, even if the earth is shaken
    and mountains fall into the ocean depths;

even if the seas roar and rage,
    and the hills are shaken by the violence.

Psalm 46:1–3

As a small stone, dropped in a pool, sends ripples to its
    furthest edges,
help us know our small actions of love and kindness
    can do great good.
Help us remember Naaman's slave girl, who spoke a
    few small words that rippled out to joy and faith and
    healing.
Help us do the good things we can,
trusting you will use them.

The Lord is my light and my salvation;
I will fear no one.
The Lord protects me from all danger;
I will never be afraid.

Psalm 27:1

Alone with none but thee, my God,
I journey on my way.
What need I fear, when thou art near
O king of night and day?
More safe am I within thy hand
Than if a host did round me stand.

St Columba (521–97)

O God,
You created us to enjoy your goodness.
You created me,
you created those I love,
and you created those who hate me
to enjoy your goodness together.

MARY JOSLIN

We, like Jonah, often find it hard to do what we know
 is right. Help us, dear Lord.
We find it hard to go to our enemies and do them good
We find it hard to forgive them, as you are willing to do
Help us to learn from your love for us, and your
 forgiveness of us. Help us trust in your great goodness

SEVEN

FAR FROM HOME

Dear God,
We have arrived at this, our new home, feeling
  as lost as windblown seeds that are dropped
  upon the earth.
Let us put down roots here where we have
  landed, and let our lives unfold in your love
  and light.

When we find ourselves somewhere strange, and new,
help us to pray for the place, and the people.
Help us to work for their good.

Try to be at
peace with
everyone,
and try to live
a holy life.

HEBREWS 12:14

Uncertainty

As the rain hides the stars,
as the autumn mist hides the hills,
as the clouds veil the blue of the sky,
so the dark happenings of my lot
hide the shining of your face from me.

Yet, if I may hold your hand in the darkness,
it is enough, since I know that,
though I may stumble in my going,
you do not fall.

GAELIC PRAYER (TRANSLATED BY ALISTAIR MACLEAN)

When all our hopes and dreams lie before us like
    heaps of dry bones,
help us to remember that you can bring breath and life
    and hope back
to even the deadest-seeming dream.

War and peace

O God,
Settle disputes among the nations,
among the great powers near and far.

FROM MICAH 4:3

Dear God,
Take care of those who live in war zones:
Afraid of noise,
afraid of silence;
Afraid for themselves,
afraid for others;
Afraid to stay,
afraid to go;
Afraid of living,
afraid of dying.
Give them peace in their hearts,
in their homes
and in their land.

When God's kingdom comes
the wolves and sheep will live together in peace,
and leopards will lie down with young goats.
Calves and lion cubs will feed together
sharing the same pasture.

Little children will take care of them
and snakes will not inflict any poison.
There will be nothing harmful or evil
and the whole world will honour God.

FROM ISAIAH 11

We thank you for the courage of Queen Esther, who
spoke out for her people even though she was afraid,
and saved many lives. Help us to know when we are
the right person in the right place to speak up for
justice and peace. Help us have courage.

Long dark nights

O God who was with Daniel, and with Shadrach,
Meshach, and Abednego, in their long night awake, be
with me this night. Send your angels to watch over me.
I will trust in your unfailing love until the dawn light
comes.

Father God,
I am awake in the night,
and all alone,
like so many others.
Some are afraid: give them courage.
Some are worried: give them hope.
Some are sad: give them comfort.
Some are just tired: give them sleep.

MARY JOSLIN

I sing a song of praise to God
throughout the darkest night,
for guarding me, for guiding me
to know what's good and right.
No evil things will frighten me,
no shadows from the tomb,
for God is light and life and power
to scatter midnight's gloom.

Based on Psalm 16:7–11

When things we have loved and worked for lie in ruins, smashed and broken, help us to be rebuilders, like Nehemiah. When people are discouraged, and have given up hope, help us encourage them, and show them that things can be mended, in your love.

EIGHT

A New Beginning — Christmas

Scatter the darkness from before our paths.

ADAPTED FROM THE ALTERNATIVE SERVICE BOOK

The days are dark.
Dear God, give us your true light.

The days are dark.
Dear God, give us your true life.

The days are dark.
Dear God, give us your true love.

We thank you for being born among us,
   sharing with us what it is to be human.
We thank you for showing us a way to live,
   full of grace and truth.
Light up our path, and let us walk with you.

FROM JOHN 1

This is what love is: it is not that we have loved God,
but that he loved us, and sent his Son.

1 JOHN 4:10

The dawn is breaking, the snow is making
everything shimmer and glimmer and white.

The trees are towering, the mist is devouring
all that is in the reaches of sight.

A bell is ringing, the town is beginning
slowly, gradually, to come to life.

A candle is lighted, and all are excited,
for today is the ending of all man's strife.

Lord Jesus,
You have given us so many rich gifts:
Let us use them to do your work in this world.

Let us remember Mary this Christmas
And may God bless our mothers.

Let us remember Joseph this Christmas
And may God bless our fathers.

Let us remember Elizabeth and Zechariah and John
  this Christmas
And may God bless all our relatives.

Let us remember the shepherds this Christmas
And may God bless all those who will be working.

Let us remember the wise men this Christmas
And may God bless all those who will be travelling.

Let us remember Jesus this Christmas
And may God bless us all and make us his children.

Gifts

Lord Jesus,
The wise men brought you gold:
Let us use our riches to do good.

The wise men brought you frankincense:
Let our prayers rise like smoke to heaven.

The wise men brought you myrrh:
Let us seek to comfort those who are sad and grieving.

Let there be little Christmases
throughout the year,
when unexpected acts of kindness
bring heaven's light to earth.

MARY JOSLIN

What can I give him,
Poor as I am?
If I were a shepherd
I would bring a lamb;
If I were a wise man
I would do my part;
Yet what I can I give him –
Give my heart.

CHRISTINA ROSSETTI (1830–94)

O God,
be to me
like the evergreen tree
and shelter me in your shade,
and bless me again
like the warm gentle rain
that gives life to all you have made.

BASED ON HOSEA 14:4–8

Love came down at Christmas,
Love all lovely, Love Divine;
Love was born at Christmas,
Star and Angels gave the sign.

Worship we the Godhead,
Love Incarnate, Love Divine,
Worship we our Jesus,
But wherewith for sacred sign?

Love shall be our token,
Love shall be yours and love be mine,
Love to God and all men,
Love for plea and gift and sign.

CHRISTINA ROSSETTI (1830–94)

NINE

LISTENING TO JESUS

John the Baptist — the call to change

Take my wrongdoing
and throw it away,
down in the deep of the sea;
welcome me into your kingdom of love
for all of eternity.

BASED ON MICAH 7:18–20

I told God everything:
I told God about all the wrong things I had done.
I gave up trying to pretend.
I gave up trying to hide.
I knew that the only thing to do was to confess.

And God forgave me.

BASED ON PSALM 32:5

Come, let us follow Jesus, who loves us.

Jesus said:

You are blessed when you know how poor you are
   inside,

for then you are open to God and his ways.

You are blessed when you are sad,

for then you will feel a loving hand on your shoulder.

You are blessed when you are gentle and humble;

you will see all of earth's good things, there for you.

You are blessed when you hunger for what is right;

you will be satisfied.

You are blessed when you live generously and kindly,

for you will be treated with kindness, too.

You are blessed when you are wholeheartedly good;

nothing will stand between you and God.

You are blessed when you work for peace;

you will be called one of God's children.

He holds all things in His right hand,
  The rich, the poor, the great, the small;
When we sleep, or sit, or stand,
  He is with us, for He loves us all.

Thomas Miller (1807–74)

Prayer

I cast my prayer on the river
and let it float to the sea
and over the far horizon
and off to eternity.

Jesus said:
Ask, and you will receive;
seek, and you will find;
knock, and the door will be opened to you.

For everyone who asks will receive,
and anyone who seeks will find,
and the door will be opened to those who knock.

Your Father in heaven will give good
things to those who ask him.

From Matthew 7:7–8,11

Our Father in heaven,
hallowed be your name,
your kingdom come,
your will be done,
on earth as in heaven.
Give us today our daily bread.
Forgive us our sins
as we forgive those who sin against us.
Lead us not into temptation
but deliver us from evil.

For the kingdom, the power,
and the glory are yours
now and for ever.
Amen.

THE LORD'S PRAYER

Some ask the world
   and are diminished
in the receiving
   of it. You gave me
only this small pool
   that the more I drink
from, the more overflows
   me with sourceless light.

R. S. THOMAS (1913–2000)

O God,
as truly as you are our father,
so just as truly you are our mother.
We thank you, God our father,
for your strength and goodness.
We thank you, God our mother,
for the closeness of your caring.
O God, we thank you for the great love
you have for each one of us.

JULIAN OF NORWICH (1342–AFTER 1416)

God feeds the birds that sing from the treetops;
God feeds the birds that wade by the sea;
God feeds the birds that dart through the meadows;
So will God take care of me?

God clothes the flowers that bloom on the hillside;
God clothes the blossom that hangs from the tree;
As God cares so much for the birds and the flowers
I know God will take care of me.

BASED ON MATTHEW 6

Learn to lend the things you own,
Learn to live with less,
Learn to look to a further shore
And God your life will bless.

MARY JOSLIN

Teach me, my God and king,
In all things thee to see,
And what I do in any thing,
To do it as for thee.

GEORGE HERBERT (1593–1633)

TEN

YOUR KINGDOM COME

Waiting

Help me to be patient as I wait for your kingdom
and your righteousness:
as patient as a farmer who trusts that the rains
will come in their season,
and that the land will produce its harvest.
Keep my hopes high.
Help me to pray to you and to praise you.

MARY JOSLIN

I wait eagerly for the Lord's help
and in his word I trust.
I wait for the Lord
more eagerly than watchmen wait for the dawn.

PSALM 130:5–6

The Kingdom of God is very near.

FROM LUKE 10:9

Prayers for the sick

We pray for someone who is sick.
May they have peace instead of pain,
strength instead of weakness,
joy instead of sorrow,
comfort instead of distress.

We thank you for all who look after those who are
    sick.
We thank you for the skill and learning of those who
understand our bodies and know how to make us well.
We thank you for those who bring food, and drinks,
laughter and little gifts, love, and a hand to hold.
Bless them, dear Lord; give them cheerfulness and
strength.

Lord Jesus,
We think of the people who brought their friend to
you, making a hole in the roof and lowering him on
ropes. We bring our friend to you now, asking for you
to heal and help them.

Dear Father God,
Today there are many children all over the world who
cannot get up because they are sick.
Some of them have been ill for a long time and have
forgotten what it is like to run and play and enjoy
games with their friends. Lord, help us to imagine
what it is like to have to stay in bed all the time, and
how lonely it must feel. Help us to think what we can
do for anyone we know who is ill.

CAROL WATSON

Table graces

Lord Jesus, who broke bread beside the lake and all
   were fed,
thank you for feeding us.
Lord Jesus, who asked his disciples to pass food to
   the crowds,
may we do the same.
Lord Jesus, who saw to it that all the spare food was
   gathered,
may we let no good thing go to waste.
Lord Jesus, who gave thanks,
we thank you now.

The bread is warm and fresh,
The water cool and clear.
Lord of all life, be with us,
Lord of all life, be near.

    AFRICAN GRACE

The Lord is good to me,
And so I thank the Lord
For giving me the things I need,
The sun, the rain, the appleseed.
The Lord is good to me.

ATTRIBUTED TO JOHN CHAPMAN, PLANTER OF ORCHARDS
(1774–1845)

Come Lord Jesus be our guest,
And may our meal by thee be blest.

ATTRIBUTED TO MARTIN LUTHER (1483–1546)

Parables

Everyday blessings
include
but are not limited to
sunrise
birdsong
silence
chatter
weeds in flower
doing good for free
a word of praise
daring
surviving
food
the homeward road
an old chair
twilight
stars.

MARY JOSLIN

We can do no great things,
Only small things with great love.

Blessed Teresa of Calcutta (1910–97)

Dear God,
When I see someone in trouble,
may I know when to stop and help
and when to hurry to fetch help;
but may I never pass by,
pretending I did not see.

Based on the parable of the good Samaritan,
Luke 10:25–37

This is what God says:

"I myself will look for my people and take care of them in the same way as shepherds take care of their sheep.

"I will bring them back from all the places where they were scattered on that dark, disastrous day.

"I will lead them to the mountains and the streams of their own land, so they may make their home amid the green pastures.

"I shall be their God, their Good Shepherd; they will be my people, my flock."

From Ezekiel 34

Lord Jesus,
Make me as kind to others
as I would want to be to you.
Make me as generous to others
as I would want to be to you.
May I take time to help them
as I would want to take time to help you.
May I take trouble to help them
as I would want to take trouble to help you.
May I look into the faces of those I meet
and see your face.

BASED ON MATTHEW 25:37–40

ELEVEN

WHO IS JESUS?

Grant me to recognize in other men, Lord God,
the radiance of your own face.

Pierre Teilhard de Chardin (1881–1955)

Help me, Lord Jesus, learn who you are.
Help me learn as I try to love, and forgive,
and help others as you did.
Thank you most of all for loving me just as I am.

You are the peace of all things calm
You are the place to hide from harm
You are the light that shines in dark
You are the heart's eternal spark
You are the door that's open wide
You are the guest who waits inside
You are the stranger at the door
You are the calling of the poor
You are my Lord and with me still
You are my love, keep me from ill
You are the light, the truth, the way
You are my Saviour this very day.

CELTIC ORAL TRADITION

Dear God,

Help me to love you with all my heart,

with all my soul and with all my mind.

Help me to love those around me as I love myself.

BASED ON THE WORDS OF JESUS FROM MATTHEW 22:34–40

O God,

Let me learn how to love.

May I grow more patient.

May I speak more kindly.

May I act more humbly.

May I never give up learning to love.

BASED ON 1 CORINTHIANS 13

Lord Jesus,
May our lives bear the mark of love.
As we are kind, as we share, as we are gentle,
may your love be seen in us.
Help us, for this is hard for us.

The road to Good Friday

Dear God,
May I welcome you as my king:
King of peace,
King of love,
King in death,
King of life.

We pray for all people who are in prison, falsely
    accused.
We pray for all who are locked away because people
in power want them silenced. Give them courage and
strength in their troubles.

O God,

Put an end to death.

Put an end to grief and crying and pain.

Make all things new.

Lead us to heaven.

FROM REVELATION 21

We give them back to you dear Lord, who gavest them
   to us.

Yet as thou didst not lose them in giving,

so we have not lost them by their return.

For what is thine is ours always, if we are thine.

QUAKER PRAYER

Lord Jesus, who died upon the cross:
You know this world's suffering,
You know this world's sorrowing,
You know this world's dying.

In your name, Lord Jesus, who rose again:
I will work for this world's healing,
I will work for this world's rejoicing,
I will work for this world's living.

Jesus, who walked to the cross,
be with us when we feel abandoned.

Jesus, who walked to the cross,
be with us when we face danger.

Jesus, who walked to the cross,
be with us when we are suffering.

When sorrow threatens to defeat us,
Jesus, who rose from the dead, be with us.

Blessed be the name of Jesus, who died to save us.

Blessed be Jesus, who had compassion on us.

Blessed be Jesus, who suffered loneliness, rejection
and pain, for our sakes.

Blessed be Jesus, through whose cross I am forgiven.

Lord Jesus, deepen my understanding of your suffering
and death.

WRITTEN BY YOUNG PEOPLE IN KENYA

Come, O Joy:

Let heaven break into my dark night of sorrow
like the early dawn of a summer morning.

TWELVE

NEW LIFE

Easter

Come, Holy Angels,
into this dark night.
Roll away the stone of death.
Let the light of life
shine from heaven.

Good Friday is locked in winter,
in grief and death and dark;
Easter Sunday begins the springtime,
rising up like the lark.

The tree of thorns
is dressed in white
for resurrection day;
and joy springs from
the underworld
now death is put away.

The whole bright world rejoices now:
with laughing cheer! with boundless joy!
The birds do sing on every bough:
Alleluia!

Then shout beneath the racing skies:
with laughing cheer! with boundless joy!
To him who rose that we might rise:
Alleluia!

God, Father, Son and Holy Ghost:
with laughing cheer! with boundless joy!
Our God most high, our joy, our boast:
Alleluia!

EASTER CAROL (17TH CENTURY)

My life flows on in endless song;
Above earth's lamentation
I hear the sweet though far-off hymn
That hails a new creation:
Through all the tumult and the strife
I hear the music ringing;
It finds an echo in my soul –
How can I keep from singing?

What though my joys and comforts die?
The Lord my Saviour liveth;
What though the darkness gather round!
Songs in the night he giveth:
No storm can shake my inmost calm
While to that refuge clinging;
Since Christ is Lord of heaven and earth,
How can I keep from singing?

ROBERT LOWRY (1826–99)

When we are sad, help us to speak of our sorrow, and hear words of hope. Help us know you walk with us, as you walked with the two on the Emmaus road. Help us to recognize you in the breaking and sharing of bread, as you warm our hearts with your joy.

Jesus' body,
Broken bread,
By God's word
We all are fed.
Jesus' lifeblood,
Wine that's spilt,
As one temple
We are built.
At this table
Take your place:
Feast upon
God's love and grace.

A PRAYER FOR HOLY COMMUNION

The olive tree I thought was dead
has opened new green leaves instead
and where the landmines tore the earth
now poppies dance with joy and mirth.

The doves build nests, they coo and sigh
beside the field where corn grows high
and grapes hang heavy on the vine,
and those who fought share bread and wine.

We celebrate Easter with the disciples who
    saw the risen Jesus,
and who knew that love was stronger than
    death.

We also remember Thomas, for whom
    Easter was a long time coming,
and all those who feel alone in their doubt
    and despair this Easter.

Risen Jesus, make yourself known to us all
    in due time
so that we may know for sure the joy of heaven.

Ascension Day

Christ has no body now on earth but yours, no hands
but yours, no feet but yours… Yours are the feet with
which he is to go about doing good, and yours are the
hands with which he is to bless us now.

St Teresa of Avila (1515–82)

Pentecost

Spirit of God
put love in my life.
Spirit of God
put joy in my life.
Spirit of God
put peace in my life.
Spirit of God
make me patient.
Spirit of God
make me kind.
Spirit of God
make me good.
Spirit of God
give me faithfulness.
Spirit of God
give me humility.
Spirit of God
give me self-control.

FROM GALATIANS 5:22–23

Evening prayers

Stay with us, Lord: the day is almost over and it is
getting dark.

FROM LUKE 24:29

Lord, keep us safe this night,
Secure from all our fears;
May angels guard us while we sleep,
Till morning light appears.

JOHN LELAND (1754–1841)

Watch, dear Lord, with those who wake, or watch, or weep tonight, and give your angels charge over those who sleep. Tend your sick ones, O Lord Christ, rest your weary ones. Bless your dying ones. Soothe your suffering ones. Pity your afflicted ones. Shield your joyous ones. And all for your love's sake.

St Augustine (354–430)

Now I lay me down to sleep,
I pray thee, Lord, thy child to keep;
Thy love to guard me through the night
And wake me in the morning light.

Traditional

Lord, behold our family here assembled.

We thank you for this place in which we dwell,

For the love that unites us,

For the peace accorded to us this day,

For the hope with which we expect the morrow;

For the health, the work, the food and the bright skies

That make our lives delightful;

For our friends in all parts of the earth.

Amen.

ROBERT LOUIS STEVENSON (1850–94)

Blessings

Deep peace of the running waves to you.
Deep peace of the flowing air to you.
Deep peace of the quiet earth to you.
Deep peace of the shining stars to you.
Deep peace of the infinite peace to you.

ADAPTED FROM ANCIENT GAELIC RUNES

The everlasting Father bless us with his blessing
everlasting.

ARCHBISHOP THOMAS CRANMER (1489–1556)

May the grace of Christ our Saviour,
And the Father's boundless love,
With the Holy Spirit's favour,
Rest upon us from above.

JOHN NEWTON (1725–1807)

May the Lord himself, who is our source of peace,
give you peace at all times and in every way. The Lord
be with you all.

2 THESSALONIANS 3:16

May God make safe to you each steep,
May God make open to you each pass,
May God make clear to you each road,
And may he take you in the clasp of his own two
hands.

FROM *CARMINA GADELICA*

Wherever you go,
May God the Father be with you.
Wherever you go,
May God the Son be with you.
Wherever you go,
May God the Spirit be with you.

May the Lord bless you,
may the Lord take care of you;
May the Lord be kind to you,
may the Lord be gracious to you;
May the Lord look on you with favour,
may the Lord give you peace.

FROM NUMBERS 6:24–26

All shall be Amen and Alleluia.
We shall rest and we shall see.
We shall see and we shall know.
We shall know and we shall love.
We shall love and we shall praise.
Behold our end which is no end.

St Augustine (354–430)

Whoever is thirsty, come and drink freely from the waters of life. It is a gift for you.

Index of First Lines

BIBLE REFERENCES

The prayers and verses in this book are collected into twelve chapters that correspond to those of the companion volume, *The Bible Story Retold in Twelve Chapters*.

Some of the prayers and verses have been based on or inspired by specific Bible stories. The Bible book and chapter references are given below in bold.

The following page reference (in italics) is to the corresponding page or section in *The Bible Story Retold in Twelve Chapters*.